Fishing The Star

Copyright 2019

Visit our website for more books
https://k-imagine-pub.com/

FreeChildren's Content, New Book Update
http://bit.ly/kid_kindle

A POLICE OFFICER, ALSO KNOWN AS AN OFFICER, POLICEMAN, POLICEWOMAN, COP/COPPER, POLICE AGENT, OR A POLICE EMPLOYEE IS A WARRANTED LAW EMPLOYEE OF A POLICE FORCE.

Police officers uphold law and order through the detection, prevention and investigation of crime.

Duties of a police officer include interviewing suspected criminals, taking statements, dealing with paperwork and many more.

The education requirement for police officer is high school diploma or equivalent, some agencies require college-level training or a degree.

Having a college degree is not a requirement for getting hired by most police departments, but it can help to have even a few years of education in a related field, especially if you plan to later become a detective or hold an administrative position

Police officer candidates must pass a physical ability test (PAT) to qualify for the force

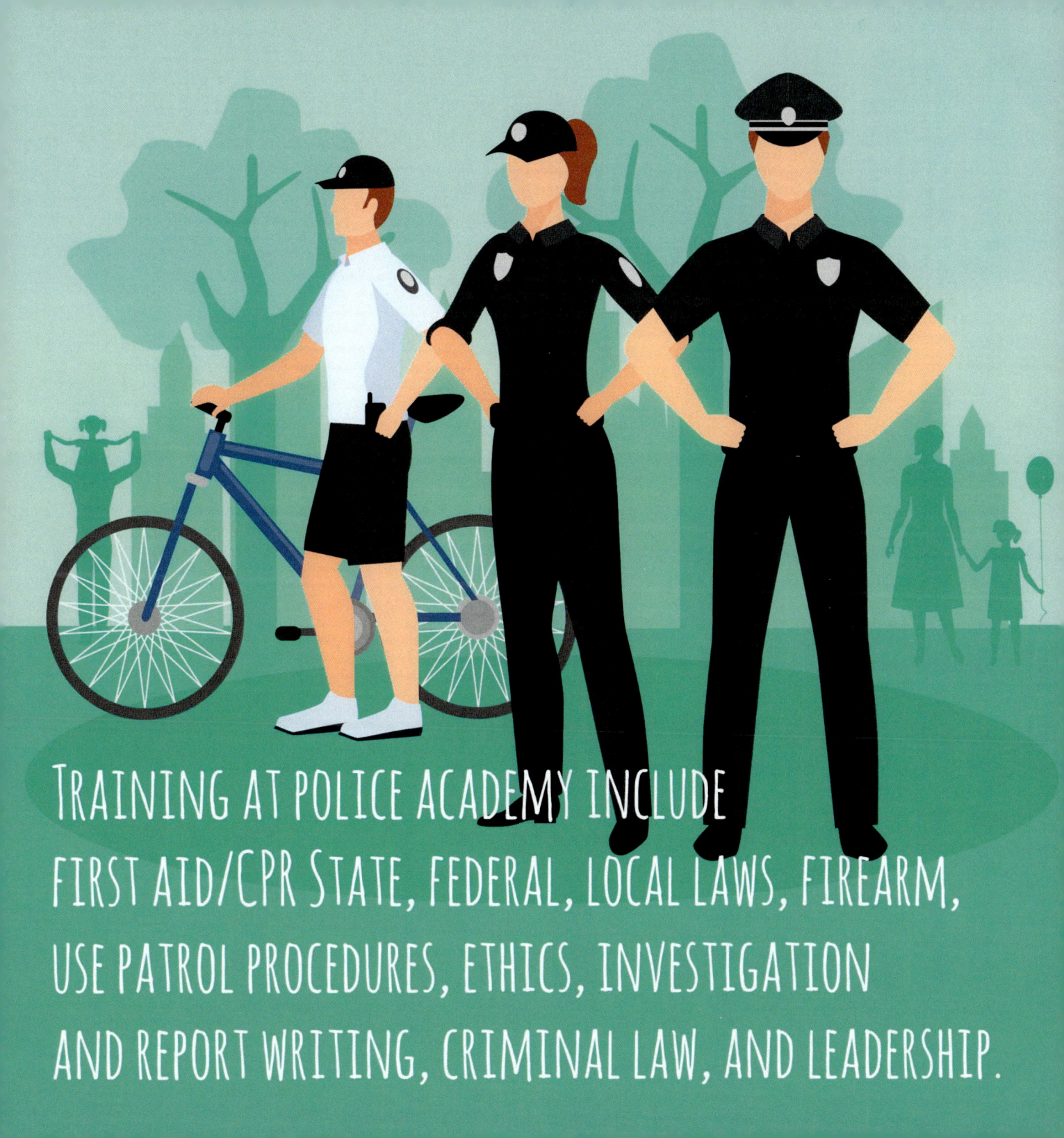

Training at police academy include first aid/CPR State, federal, local laws, firearm, use patrol procedures, ethics, investigation and report writing, criminal law, and leadership.

In order to gain a position on the police force, candidates are required to pass examination to ensure competence.

Most divisions also administer physical tests of strength, vision, hearing and agility.

Some units conduct psychiatric or background interviews to assess a recruit's personal characteristics and overall suitability for a career in law enforcement

Projected job growth for a police officer in 2014-2024 is 5%.

The median salary for 2015 was $58,320.

The age requirement for police officer is 18. Applications can be accepted at the age of 18.

A number of crimes will mean a definite or likely rejection of your application, including anyone who has received a formal caution in the last five years, committed a violent crime or public order offence.

In large police departments, new recruits receive 12-14 weeks of training through their own in-house academy.

A police officer career is suited to anyone who thrives on challenge.

Most aspiring police officer pursue degrees in criminal justice..

IN DIFFERENT COUNTRIES, POLICE OFFICERS ARE GIVEN DIFFERENT EQUIPMENT TO DEAL WITH THE CRIME THAT IS IN THEIR COUNTRY.

Officers must be able to run long distances, sprint quickly to catch suspects, and use physical force to detain or subdue people when necessary.

The average police officer salary in America in 2012 was $56,980 per year.

When you apply to become a police officer, the department will run a credit check as part of your background check, and you will be penalized if your score is low.

Most police officers work outdoors while on patrol, and are subjected to all types of weather conditions.

Most police jobs are not publicly advertised.

Made in the USA
Las Vegas, NV
24 November 2020